YOU.

The Real State of Life

Austin Bergman

Luxury Real Estate Mogul & Realist

You. The Real State of Life

MTE Publishing
mtepublishing.com

Special Thanks & Acknowledgements

My mom always instructed me to say these three phrases: please, thank you, and I'm sorry. Please, will turn a demand into a request. Thank you, shows appreciation and gratitude. I'm sorry, means we take ownership of our actions...we may or may not get a do-over with an apology… so, walk away knowing this.

So, *thank you* for investing in my literary work. You are about to embark upon an exciting journey of discovering the power of understanding your truth and transparency. If you know someone who is on a journey of true self-acceptance, purchase a copy and gift it to them.

I apologize to my former self for not knowing how to handle my truth. I was reckless and a butt. I apologize to those I hurt on my journey to becoming my best self. I hope this opens a door for peace and healing to reside.

Please share a review of my literary work on Amazon and follow me on social media: The Real State of Life!

Be YOU Authentically,

Austin Bergman, Realist & Luxury Real Estate Mogul

Foreword

By Betsy Pepine, Founder & CEO of Pepine Reality

I have always been drawn to people who have both the curiosity and courage to discover and be their authentic selves. As human beings, we feel pressure to live under the structure, constraints, and expectations of the groups into which we are born. Familiar, religious, and cultural organizations each, overtly and not so overtly, tell us who we are and how to behave, in order to gain acceptance. As we become older and choose a career, we have additional roles and codes of conduct imposed on us, again, many not to our choosing.

Sadly, many of us go through our lives never questioning these rules and roles. Some of us are oblivious to these roles, while others recognize them and accept them as "what is," permanent or too hard to change.

As a fellow real estate broker in Florida, I admire Austin for his courage in his journey to live an authentic life, even when it is in opposition to the expectations of those around him. When we go against the norms and expectations of the society in which we live, we confront our greatest fear(s) head-on. As social beings, rejection is one of our biggest fears. Our survival and propagation of our species hinges on our ability to work together and form meaningful and beneficial relationships.

Fear of being cast out from our social circles may not seem daunting but imagine having to choose between living as your authentic self or maintaining the status quo, in an effort (not guaranteed) to be accepted by your family, children, colleagues, clients, friends, and society at large. Every day, many of us choose the latter, because it *seems* to be the road that is easier to travel. When we choose to live our lives under a set of beliefs we don't espouse, or in a body we cannot fully embrace, or with partners we know are not right for us… these decisions cause us to deny ourselves and forsake our right to exude *real* happiness and peace.

Join Austin as he shares his story of authenticity and courage, I believe you will be inspired to live your *most* authentic life, too!

Table of Contents

Introduction:
My Not-So-Funny Valentine

The happiness I portrayed was a facade. My life was an exquisite house but in reality, things were headed into foreclosure from the start. We had the money, and we could afford the dream. There is a vast difference between buying what we can afford and having the ability to maintain it. Some things will cost much more than money can buy because the value is priceless. Although, money can buy the appearance of what we want people to believe and accept... there is no freedom in true lies.

I was drawn into the reality of who I was meant to be when I witnessed how other gay men lived. I wanted to be gay. I needed to be who I was so that I could be happy. There is a magnetism inside of each of us that draws us to what and who we are destined to be. I was tired because I was building a life, but I wanted to live my true self. Unfortunately, where our energy goes, our mind typically follows.

However, I was afraid that I was going to lose everything coupled with rejection. The certainty is, if I stayed, I would still be called Mr. Valentine to someone.

When we pretend, our lives will never be what they are supposed to be until we live our lives authentically. Trust this fact: Authenticity equates to freedom. I was somewhat free [which means I was locked up in the prison of life]. Life isn't supposed to be a prison, it's a surprise party [those are the best kind]. I had it all but had nothing at the same time. I had a wife, family, and money but happiness was nowhere in sight. I couldn't see it, hear it, or feel it. Most importantly, I couldn't be it.

The older I got, the more settled I became with staying in versus "coming out". I was OK with this because I didn't want to be uncomfortable. I've learned that YOU have to become uncomfortable to be comfortable and free. The discomfort is temporary but real happiness lasts a lifetime [it's an inside job]. So, I stopped denying who I was and realized I had to rebuild from the ground up... If YOU are going to build anything, YOU may as well build what YOU want and need. Our needs supersede our wants. I had to be Austin Bergman because Mr. Valentine was never who I was or meant to be. Put some respect on my name.

I decided I would no longer be trapped inside myself... scared and depressed. I refused to hide any longer. We can only run and hide for so long. My authentic self was bound to erupt, purposely.

The danger in it all is giving into the lie of believing that I'd lose everything, an effort to do just one thing and that was to be me. So, I did it, I came out and I am a great person independent of friendships, networks, social status, achievements, and accolades. Greatness is inside of us regardless of how life happens to us.

So, when I came out, I had to conduct a self-appraisal of myself and discovered the value of my life and I flipped it upside down and decided to be who I am from the inside out. I threw myself a life upside down and increased my life expectancy. This is where I discovered happiness. Yes, my life is a little fucked up [nobody's perfect] but I am happy! Content with my kids, making money, and most importantly the peace and in that order. I took the expectation off people [for acceptance] and became who I longed to be.

I recommend building from the ground up. Make sure your foundation is not built on lies, that's like quicksand [you're bound to be swallowed up alive] or even worse, the walking dead. Build your foundation on truth, it's like settled cement; nothing can move it [except an act of God].

I am Austin Bergman, a gay man, who loved her, but I decided to love myself more. Some may call it selfishness but there's nothing selfish about loving and accepting everything about YOU. Furthermore, when we don't accept who we are, oftentimes, it's because other people are uncomfortable with who we are and who they are. We cannot live up to other people's expectations, we must live up to our own. This is how we become our best selves, we learn to accept and love ourselves. Love brings out the best in us... It's a powerful force. So, stop buying the dream and start living the reality. YOU... That's the real state of life!

"A person's success in life can be measured by the number of uncomfortable conversations he or she is willing to have."

~Tim Ferris

Chapter 1

We Always Knew

I grew up in Chesterfield, VA., a small conservative town that thrives on the construction industry. It's somewhat redneckish and the townspeople are closed minded. Nevertheless, my mom always knew...most moms do. She caught me with gay porn. I had even brought guys home. In high school, I was the "pretty boy" who was well dressed and drove a BMW. I didn't play sports and I didn't like getting sweaty. I despised PE because I did not want to shower because I was afraid I'd be aroused. Therefore, I knew I was gay around 15.

Nevertheless, I tried to be "normal" to fit in. That meant going to prom with girls, dating girls and being with girls. However, I was attracted to both [girls and boys]. This stage was confusing because being normal meant being accepted. My ex even caught me on the computer watching gay porn. When I denied the truth of who I was, I essentially set myself up to live in hell [right here on earth]. It was like being locked up in my own solitary confinement.

I was born and raised Catholic; although not practicing. We only attended mass at Christmas. My childhood was rough because my dad was an alcoholic and there was a lot of domestic violence in the home; he beat my mom more times that I can count. This is one of the reasons why I suppressed my authentic identity, because love and acceptance [seemingly] didn't exist in my home.

I met my ex-wife when I was 17, the summer of 2000. We hung out every single day before she left for New York City. I went off to culinary school in Richmond. With the tragic events of 2001 (9/11 the US terrorist attacks), she returned home while I still lived with my parents but needed my own space away from the dysfunction, so I sold my BMW to come up with the down payment on the house. I still didn't make enough money and needed a co-signer. So she agreed to co-sign for me. We used the family realtor but he didn't provide us with the "white glove" home-buying experience. That's when we decided to become realtors and change the game.

We lived together for five years during that time, she got pregnant but we aborted the baby we named Iris, which means rainbow. We managed to get through it and we never talked about it again; however, we mourned the death of the baby. Then again, I thought I didn't need a baby, at the time, because we were young and inexperienced. In retrospect, had I known how cool it is to be a father, I would have kept our baby. Two years later we got married because her parents were strict Southern Baptist and frowned upon us cohabitating.

In a matter of years, we attained great success as licensed realtors. In fact, we were considered the hottest real estate couple in Chesterfield, VA. We were out-selling everyone in the office and eventually became real estate moguls. Right before we were married, the rumors about my sexual identity continued to surface. I fought them down and she fought them down, too. I was living the dream in a suit [better known as my shield], driving an escalade and flying in private airplanes. I had the "American dream" along with a trophy wife and two beautiful children. However, I still knew I wasn't like other guys who liked watching football.

The rumors that I had slept with men continued but we still got married. Although our marriage was a train wreck waiting to happen, it was the *right* thing to do. On our wedding day, I scanned the guests at our outdoor wedding, and I realized he was there. This was the man I had a relationship with, but I still married her and she still married me; even though her girlfriend told her about the rumors she heard about me sleeping with him. Life got busy and we refused to face the truth. Everything seemed to happen all at once and the lie we lived became our truth. If we live a lie long enough, eventually we believe it's our reality.

Unfortunately, after conducting a personal comparative marketing analysis, I realized that I didn't measure up or possess the same value as the people I surrounded myself with. They withheld their truth because so many people "knew" but wouldn't grant me permission to just be me. Like in real estate, a comparative marketing analysis allows realtors to assess the value of properties in an area to derive the cost of the home that is in question [for acquisition].

In this case, the home in question is me. Truth is, no one is responsible for our value [not even "yes people"]. They will know the truth about us; however, we must seek the truth for ourselves and courageously live in it. This requires repositioning ourselves authentically, which increases our value and defines our worth. So we must get rid of the unqualified buyers in our lives... they will never invest in who we are because they don't understand the value of personal investment. Lies are costly, but the truth is priceless; especially, when that truth is connected to our liberation. I encourage YOU to conduct your own personal comparative marketing analysis so that YOU can wisely assess YOUR value. This is how I became the real Austin Bergman.

You might have to fight a battle more than once to win it."

~Margaret Thatcher

Chapter 2

Something Was Right

We had the "look" of perfection and total success. We had what everyone else dreamed of. We had it all. Everything was perfect [seemingly]: my wife, our daughters, our home, our wealth and elaborate vacations. Everything was beautiful except the truth.

Also, in our perfect but imperfect world, everyone gets married, settles down but it wasn't who I was [it was who "they" expected me to be]. It was right for social acceptance but everyone else's expectations were not for me and that's when I realized money cannot buy or replace truth, authenticity, peace or happiness. The market [and our marriage] was booming from 2004-2008. Everyone could buy a house. We were like Ken and Barbie taking center stage. Everyone would say to us we were superstars. It was prefacing our future, which was to rise to the top. We allowed everyone to buy into our narrative of success.

Then one day, our first broker, Linda Harris, sat us down and asked if we wanted to take things to the next level. We named the company and decided a heart would be our logo. It was cute. However, as much as I really didn't like the name, I relented because it was about the marketability of the brand. So we started the company and I was assigned the vice president position. December 2007 we took a leap right as a recession was on the horizon. It was the height of the subprime mortgage boom. Almost every time we blinked we sold a house; the art of selling homes came natural to us.

Between November 2007 and March 2008, we experienced the roughest part of the recession while starting our company. February 2008, our first daughter, Aveda, was born. She made her debut in the middle of the real estate market crashing. There we were with a new baby and no money! WTF! I had no deals and everything was drying up. I remember sitting in the hospital and ordering extra food that I charged to the insurance.

During this time, several of my friends committed suicide and many lost their homes. That's when I became an extremely good at short sales. As realtors, we had never experienced a recession. Nevertheless, we kept pressing forward. I put everything on my Discover card because without it, we weren't discovering anything! We started taking market share through short sales by helping people who were losing their homes to avoid foreclosure.

My first daughter gave us something to work toward. I remained loyal to my marriage, our daughter and the business. I wanted to focus on what was driving us. I had zero dollars but a whole lot of sense! Mortgage companies didn't know what was happening as the market tanked, but I knew exactly what to do. Nevertheless the marriage ended up being just about business; however, we'd have sex to celebrate our closings. As a result we had two beautiful daughters. I became such a girl dad. I'd drop them off at pre-school, pick them up and we'd take daddy-daughter dates at a local yogurt shop.

My oldest daughter Veta Beta, is pretty and name-brand driven and Artie Party is also pretty but she's the eccentric one. As their father, my goal was to take them to a different country every year. We would catch a private plane, get on a helicopter then be driven up to the vacation home we were renting. On one occasion, I made a wager with the pilot to land the helicopter between two palm trees. Everybody freaked out, and argued that it was impossible. They were wrong, because we're all still here.

We took a vacation to Caye Caulker, an island off the coast of Belize. By the middle of the week we learned what poverty was. We met a braider and her daughter showed up naked and breast-feeding. My daughter said, "We're leaving our luggage for them." And that's what we did.

One of the funniest memories I have with my children is our trip to the Bahamas. On the way there, we flew in first-class pods. On our return trip back to the states, we had regular first-class seats and not the pods. At the sight of our "regular" seats [not pods], my youngest daughter threw a temper tantrum and screamed, "I want a new plane, and my lay down bed! I am never flying "back-class" again!" At that moment, I realized I created a little monster. Nevertheless, money allowed us to create beautiful memories and expose our children to the world.

Then in 2017, after a business trip to Texas, I was hit with divorce papers. We decided to go to dinner at Capital Grill. Fortunately, her back was to the window and I saw that we were next a gay bar. Although I tried not to look in that direction of the drag queens and guys going into the bar, I couldn't resist my urge to look, my eyes kept wandering. Her eyes followed mine, and they were not following her. By that time what was left of our marriage had tanked. We couldn't tolerate each other any longer. I guess I was hoping she'd take more from me. And just like the real estate market runs in cycles [going from up ticks and booming to crashes] so did my marriage when I chose to live life and define success the way society defines it.

I know that the journey we'll all go through, will eventually throw us a curveball and how we navigate around the curves is called life. Everything was gravy until the recession hit. Tough times determine who we really are. When it was good, it was good but when it was bad, holy shit! Nevertheless, shit also makes the best fertilizer. Shit continued to happen when the IRS (the international relocation service) of all entities, came after me because I owed taxes. My accounts and all of my assets were frozen.

Lesson: Social acceptance and expectation lead us into a constant facade, be who YOU are and NOT who "they" expect or want YOU to be or you'll end up hating yourself!

Side Note (SN): Just because we have a history with someone or something…. This doesn't mean we continue to live with it or them as our reality. We must refuse to bury our heads in the dirt while our asses are exposed! My failure to accept who I was caused me to keep my head in the dirt. I was tired of getting dirty at least like that!

"Sometimes shit has to happen for shit to happen."

~ Austin Bergman

Chapter 3

Nasty in the Backseat

There, I said it…"I'm gay." It was no secret; I guess I needed to confess in that heated moment to be heard and legitimately recognized as such. I spent the night in jail. Who would have thought confessing that I'm gay would get me locked up...go figure. Actually, what started out as an intense verbal exchange turned into a nasty physical altercation in the backseat of our Lincoln Navigator. We both were pretty beat up, but me being the "man" I was carried off in handcuffs.

It was at the point that I began to dissect our entire marriage. I realized that we were living a toxic life from the start that involved both physical and verbal abuse. We were the slumlords of our estate and the property value had depreciated greatly.

We met at the Brandermill Inn, a beautiful resort. It's also where I had a couple flings. Nevertheless, through the years, the venue deteriorated and she'd say, "There's our marriage, it's deteriorating away." Eventually the facility was bulldozed. The property was used to reconstruct another beautiful retirement community. How ironic...talk about irony? Words are powerful but the truth is powerful and liberating. I realized I had to rebuild myself from the ground up.

My ex was demeaning and the abuse was ongoing. I had to keep my mouth shut and remain her trophy husband. She belittled my family and referred to them as drunks and skanks. She was a screamer, and screaming is a natural self-defense mechanism. When she did this, I told her, "You're losing the argument, that's why you're screaming." My ideas had no value to her. It was always her way or no way. She often told me, "Never burn a bridge, just stop using it because YOU will need it again down the road!" Everything and everyone was disposable and had to serve to her benefit. When we had staff meetings, I was told to keep my mouth shut, so I complied because I was afraid of her fury. When she unleashed, she UNLEASHED! She controlled everything so much so that our younger daughter didn't meet my parents until she was almost two-years-old. I was called an idiot because I didn't finish college. Simply put, she was an independent bully. Her outburst often resulted in me going back and apologizing for her obnoxious behavior.

I remember we were at a teacher appreciation event that we sponsored. However, I was late and as I walked in she said, "Shut the fuck up, stand there, and look pretty!" I left, and my walk off was beautiful and unapologetic. Although we tried not to fight in front of the kids, sadly it happened. There were physical altercations on both sides and I realized the abuse wouldn't stop until we ended our mascarade of marital bliss. It was no secret that our marriage was dysfunctional on so many levels. However, neither of us had the guts to call it quits but our facade of being "successful" seemed to be more valuable,at the time.

Nevertheless, I realized we must be great property managers/stewards of everything that we choose to invest in, particularly our relationships. We invested in everyone's relationship except our own. That is how we built our wealth through relationships. When an investment takes a downturn and continues to spiral out of control, own your part in it, but leave... especially, when things become unsafe. We are the tenants of relationships and it must be a true partnership, in which respect and transparency are the cornerstones. This serves true in all relationships: personal, friendships, and in business.

So here's what I did. I decided to own my bullshit, all of it. I OWNED the fact that I was young and reckless. I owned my dishonesty [with myself and others] and my willingness to place more value on a lifestyle of wealth, instead of a life of truth. I apologize to my former self [and the people I hurt in the process] for not being man enough to man up and walk away *sooner*. For not celebrating my identity and living a lie that I thought *would* sustain me.

Coming out *almost* cost me everything, but I gained a new sense of self-worth when I embraced my authentic identity. Yes, I had to return to the drawing board and when I did, I realized that not even the abuse/ trauma or anything else could minimize my greatness.

Truth is, the truth hurts really bad, but it also has the capacity to heal if we allow ourselves to own it. Additionally, when we fail to live in our truths, we're taking a backseat to our own lives. We have to be in the driver's seat even when we don't know where we're going or what may be coming ahead. We'll figure it out as we go.

The evolution of the real Austin Bergman was quite shitty at the onset. I fucked up the white picket fence vision and I was no longer invested in it. I didn't want it because I couldn't maintain it. It cost too much, I was done playing the part.

Lesson: Our truth changes the vision we have for ourselves and others, but we have to learn it's OK to have a fresh one. However, it doesn't come without processing the shit, admitting he shit, owning the shit and trying to heal from the shit. Truthfully, we're embarrassed by it, but we cannot allow shame to supersede our own need to be transparent with ourselves and others. This causes true liberation and this is how YOU become YOU...be YOU!

"Stop shrinking to fit into places you've outgrown."

~ Unknown

Chapter 4

Just Get Comfortable Being YOU

Life is a combination of both sunshine and rainbows as well as storms and rain. I have experienced my share of life's worst storms and its best sunrises. While I was married, I focused on building a real estate empire and establishing relationships with clients and potential clients to maintain a financial status that was suitable for a celebrity. Partying, drinking, and illicit drug use were my poisons of choice, and I entertained myself with these things to mask my unhappiness and hide my true self.

One day I decided to look at myself… for real. I won't say that I reveled in my looks, but I will admit that I cringed at my reflection. I had ignored him for far too long. The face looking back at me was not the face that everyone else saw. I had been hiding from myself and everyone around me. It was time for me to get comfortable with who I was, but more importantly who I needed to be. I realized that as I matured, I became more comfortable with who I was destined to be. I was not supposed to be an overweight, man-boob having, drug-using, rich guy with no purpose who was sadly waiting to come alive.

When I understood this, I took a dive into the intricacies of who I am, where I came from, and where I was going. My entire family suffered from alcoholism and sadly I almost surrendered to the seemingly innate detriment of drug abuse and alcohol as well. I had a wake-up call in 2011 after Mama Zet (my beloved grandmother) passed away from cirrhosis. She hid her fatal illness from all of us. No one knew except her.

During the Christmas holidays, Mama Zet started coughing up blood. The scene was petrifying and I felt completely helpless. I didn't want to believe my grandmother's life had been claimed by a disease that was totally preventable. A day that was supposed to be filled with joy, love, and laughter quickly turned into a day my entire family desperately wanted to forget. However, death has a way of sobering us up instantly. It makes us evaluate what is most important while forcing us to change for the better, if we want to. Fortunately, I made the decision to change right then. I couldn't continue to be a hopeless alcoholic in search of true happiness because all I had to do was look within myself to find it. And this is what I did.

In January of 2012, I asked a friend, who was a personal trainer, to help me. He responded, "I am not going to waste my time with YOU because I know YOU will not pay attention." I shifted my life and my mentality, and I became intentional regarding my health. So, I stopped drinking alcohol, changed my eating habits, and became a gym rat. I proved myself right and made a believer out of my trainer and my naysayers. When I became comfortable "being me," I was able to embrace the reality of who I was without feeling ashamed. I evolved into Austin Bergman and I crucified Mr. Valentine.

My mental space was consumed with improving myself, especially the way people perceived me. My former mentality caused me to desire the limelight, a grandiose lifestyle, and made me believe the ridiculous notion that a $1,600 suit could camouflage my identity and protect me from those who wouldn't accept me. That's bullshit. I realized underneath all of the layers of designer clothes and superficial connections, Austin Bergman was trying to claw his way out a self-made abyss of utter emptiness. From this point, I decided I didn't just want what was best for me, I needed what was best for me and so did my children, my ex-wife, my clients, and the future me.

In the process of my personal evolution, I was gripped by fear. I was convinced I would lose everything. Nevertheless, I knew I had to bulldoze the life I built and start over with a fresh foundation. Truth and honesty were my demolition tools of choice. I stopped hiding my attraction to men and I acted on it. I finally admitted the affair I had because lying to myself and the people that mattered only caused more damage. I had enough and although my evolution was painful, it was liberating! I loved being Austin Bergman, the happy gay dude. Surprisingly, those who actually cared about me, loved me too! I guess it's safe to say, the grass was greener on the other side where I was unrestrained to be me, authentically.

Lesson: Just get comfortable being YOU. Although, it may be frightening initially, your fears will subside as YOU embrace yourself. Fear is an imposter. Courage is the real thing. So, as we fearfully move forward, courage takes over and allows us to take flight on a jet plane and never turn back.

Everyone wants to ride with you in the limo, but what you want is someone who will take the bus with you when the limo breaks down.

~ Oprah Winfrey

Chapter 5

Changing Faces, Changing Circles

Whether one is engulfed in rags or riches, our circumstances are not the ultimate dictator of our destiny, we are. In June 2016, I confessed that I cheated [with a guy], it was catastrophically purposeful. This was approximately 16 years from the time we started dating. Unbeknownst to me, a year and half after my confession, she had everything appraised and I was fired from the company that I started in my garage.

Fatefully, I went from having more than enough money to do anything with to less than $8K in the bank. I signed her agreement with zero negotiation. The tides were turning and it was painfully freeing. It's interesting how we become immune to toxic and dysfunctional people or things that don't serve our betterment. There was a lot of abuse but from the outside looking in, it was awesome. However, if we are going to be honest, there are too many people who hate their jobs, hate the person they're with, and ultimately hate their lives, too. I used to be one of them because wealth is great but I realized my freedom is priceless.

Relationships are categorized by time, money and energy. If there is no reciprocity, then leave them. When I came out, people slammed doors in my face. These individuals were family members, so-called friends and clients. Initially my circle of support was countless, I mean I thought there were a lot of people who accepted and supported me, but when I revealed my true sexuality I could count my real friends on one hand. These were individuals I helped start businesses, get over humps, bailed out of bad business deals because I wanted to help them and when I needed someone to lean on, there were only a few. Those in the crowds and on my VIP list were nowhere to be found. My phone stopped ringing, my calls weren't returned and neither were text messages, and none of them helped me financially *at all.*

Reality started to sink in but I knew I would be OK; because when our backs are against the wall those of us who are determined to get out… we will relentlessly claw our way through the wall… and I did just that. I made things OK.

I lived my life one day at a time. I took a social media sabbatical. I had to find the faith to live again and dream a new dream. I embraced the reality that having a few good friends was better than a thousand fake friends anyway. I focused on those who stayed and new opportunities. In December 2017, I decided to leave Virginia. I had a new lease on life!

So I relocated to south Florida. There are so many better places to live our lives openly. I left Virginia as a real estate shark, and I was perceived as a real estate guppy in Florida… no one knew me! Nevertheless, I networked my ass off every single day for more than a year to rebuild myself and my business, the Austin Bergman way.

Equity isn't typically thought of in a personal sense. However, when the time comes for us to improve our lives we must assess our relationships, our surroundings, and the intention of our efforts. I came to this conclusion after failing forward. So, I embraced my failures, learned from my successes, and I started over. There I was living in a 400-square foot apartment, 15 suitcases packed with clothes, and my 2017 Cadillac Escalade; I was already down, so there was nowhere for me to go, except up.

I realized a lot of the agents in the area were far too relaxed so I was selective about who I spent my time with because I was determined to be a luxury realtor. I understood that I couldn't target properties that were less than $1.6 million dollars. I serve millionaires; this is my target clientele. I realized it takes just as much energy and effort [and sometimes even less] to sell a $300K home as it does to sell a $2 million home. Therefore, I will not pursue what I don't want. The ball is in my court and I am committed to working smarter, not harder and building the life I want, my way.

Now I believe in setting the standard high. We owe it to ourselves to picture what we want and fearlessly pursue it! Living authentically and purposely is awesome. Never allow someone else's perceived value of YOU to determine how YOU see yourself! Deny them access when YOU sense there isn't any true loyalty; because when they refuse to accept who YOU are, this indicates that they value the personal benefit of YOU pretending to be someone else.

I will never forget those who partied with me when I was up. These were people who would send us business for their benefit. When the bottom fell out those I would catch a bullet for were the ones with their finger on the trigger. I was shocked by who was left standing, but I couldn't stay in that place and this reality check felt as though I'd been pimp-slapped! Everything I worked for was stripped from me, even my voice and my side of the story. I had no control of the narrative but what I eventually decided was to create a new narrative. I had to grieve, forgive and move forward, but it wasn't that easy.

January 2018, I sold my first home listed at $3M. I laughed in disbelief because I couldn't believe that I pulled the deal off *by myself!* The deal was written out on a napkin. Sidenote: Anytime someone puts their signature on anything, it's legal and binding. It was in that moment when I became intentional about going after what I wanted, personally and professionally. While it took almost a year to close my first multi-million dollar deal, the lessons I learned were clear: dream big, love what YOU do, work hard, be an expert, seek peace, be honest and most importantly, be YOU!

My goal is to live an authentic life for the rest of my life. This means, I go after what I want, I surround myself with people who genuinely care about me as a human being. Today, I'm a luxury realtor who only executes contracts north of a million dollars.

Lesson: Ultimately, I learned that my most valuable asset was my authentic self. I was no longer weighed-down with the need to lie about who I am so that I would be accepted. When we are no longer hiding or pretending, we can use that same energy to maximize our potential, exponentially, and change our destiny!

The best way to be happy with someone is to learn to be happy with yourself.

~Austin Bergman

Chapter 6

Coming Out to Come Up

As a teenager, I knew I was gay. However, my apprehension came from hearing my parents and friends talk badly about gay people. Homosexuals were never addressed by their names only derogatory terms like sissy, faggot, or queer. When I was 16, I got my ears pierced. My mom had a whole cow and chased me out of the house and she asked me, "Are you a faggot, are you gay?" Her tone said "I know but I just need you to tell me."

Moms always know, nothing about their children is ever a "secret" to them. My mom used to hang out with gay people all the time, so I didn't know what the big deal was about me being gay. However, before she died, I finally got the courage to tell her what she already knew about my sexuality.

As a child/teenager, I couldn't reveal or embrace my true identity! There was no way, I would come out and be identified as gay because I knew immediate rejection was inevitable, because I was different from the majority. Who confidently says, I am gay? Nobody... I just wanted to be accepted. When who we are is deemed unacceptable to the people who are supposed to love us, we will conform to keep their love, and lie to ourselves.

A friend recommended that I keep a journal to get out my emotions. So I followed his advice. I wrote in my journal almost every day before my ex read my entries. Journaling was a form of self-prescribed therapy. I had conversations with God and myself about how He wired me. I didn't like it, in fact, I hated it because I was working so hard to be someone else instead of just being who He made me to be.

When I thought about "coming out," I asked myself [in my journal]... "Is this really who I am?"

"Am I ready for the aftermath of my open confession?" "Will my truth really bring the liberation I am seeking?" I answered all of the previous questions with a simple response. "Fuck it, it is what it is, my life can't get any worse." So when I decided to snatch the Band-Aid off, that's when I accepted who I was becoming. I also became even more aware of the innate greatness within me.

I realized the only person who could stop me was ME! I got out of my own way, and although it took me a while to simply embrace "*The Real Austin Bergman*" the journey to becoming ME was worth every tear, every triumph, every tragedy, and most importantly the lessons I have learned over time.

The small-town mentality of Chesterfield, VA would never accept the real Austin Bergman. So I lived the lie for 35 years and didn't come out publicly until I left Virginia. For years, I worked to conform to be accepted; it was a full-time job (mentally, emotionally and physically). I had to look and act straight. Fortunately, my life unraveled. I had to admit that I was unfaithful and selfish, so things had to play out the way they did or I'd still be portraying the lie of a fairytale story while living a nightmare.

Fear is the culprit that violently robs us of our ability and courage to be *who* we are and achieve what we *must*. Everyone has a coming out story. It's like a tornado forming in the ocean. First, there's the warning (what we see and know). The watch is what we expect so we proceed with caution. For those who survive, this is not a choice, it is how we are wired. There's no conversion therapy, not even Marilyn Monroe could make me go back to the life I lived.

We are normal people who are different because we are supposed to be. As a parent, I understand my primary responsibility is to accept and love my children just the way they are. This is easy for me because I am uniquely wired, and if my daughter told me she was gay or that she wanted to be a nun; I would give her a high-five for living her life the way God designed it to be!

I relocated to south Florida, where I could unapologetically be me and be accepted. It cost me everything, but it gave me the opportunity to live life on my terms. When I lived the lie, my life was "good" but now that I am living "my truth," life just continues to get better and better! I encourage others to ditch the shit and go for it. Be OK with rejection and forgive those who rejected YOU, then embrace acceptance and those who accept YOU.

After coming out, come up and BE the BEST at being YOU no matter how painful it may be. We MUST acknowledge the junk, accept that it is what it is, and intentionally pursue our destiny. We cannot get stuck coasting on the mediocrity of other people's vision for our life. The world has plenty of average people doing average things. However, there's a desperate need for more kick-ass people accomplishing incredible things and it starts with YOU being YOU!

Lesson: Everybody is different and it is up to each and everyone of us to accept that. Hatred is taught, but being different is necessary. Therefore, it is left up to us to recognize our shortcomings, judgemental behaviors, and navigate our moral compass so we do not become what we despise. The greatest part of this lesson is saying, "hatred ends with me." When this happens it isn't passed down to our children or theirs.

Your potential is endless, go and do what

you were created to do.

~Austin Bergman

Chapter 7

Self-Acceptance:
Get to Know the New YOU

Get acclimated with the new YOU. There's an adjustment period after snatching off the Band-Aid, and it may take a while for you to heal. Life will be cold as hail initially, and although the sunlight may be visible, as YOU readjust to who you are, your focus might get distorted. However, when you open your eyes to the reflection of truth in front of you... the journey gets easier because now your vision isn't obscured by your own bullshit.

I remember the first time I went into the grocery store as a divorced man, I stood in the middle of the store and cried. I made my way back to my car to compose myself. It was overwhelming. I was literally trying to pick up the pieces of my life after doing a 180 degree turn. I was vulnerable and fragile. At the same time, my life was a balancing act. I was getting to know who I was while living in this new-found freedom and I felt afraid. Life is hard and we have to make hard choices. I couldn't turn back, turning back was off the table. I couldn't remain stagnant because I knew there was greatness inside of me that wouldn't let me rest. And going forward, to my surprise, was a lot harder than I anticipated.

Fortunately, I *still* decided to move forward and not backwards. Unfortunately, too many people transitioning in life get stuck between gathering the pieces and moving forward. It's like postpartum depression and some people don't survive this phase after making a major life decision.

After we STOP hiding and remove the mask, there is a purifying freedom in openly being who we are. Authenticity is a God-given gift to us. It's a gift that very few people truly accept or are brave enough to unwrap [because sometimes beneath the layers of greatness there is also natural shittiness]… this is why we have so many imposters! Being authentically YOU, will illuminate every space that you grace, and as AWESOME as it is to be unique, there will be people who HATE you because you're YOU… and nothing like them. I didn't start embracing my light until in my 20s. I could meet someone one time and they would remember me. However, life happens and I lost it, temporarily. So I had to strive to get back to my authentic self. We have to ask ourselves, what did God put inside of us that we never had to work at? The it factor is YOU! Whether YOU are loud, funny, blunt or truthful, this is who YOU are! So the question is, who are You hiding and who do YOU need to become? Where are YOU and where are YOU headed?

This balancing act requires transparency, vulnerability, and the ability to be OKAY with YOU even if no one else is. The rejection will still be there, but do not own how others feel about YOU. Other people's problem with you is their problem, NOT yours! So STOP trying to be the person you believe other people want You to be and just be who God made you to be. When we are who we are, we don't have to sugarcoat who we are for anybody, especially those who are obviously dissatisfied with themselves. If they were content with themselves, they would not be so ridiculously consumed with YOU *being* YOU.

- Be Unforgettable
- Be Genuine
- Be Unapologetic
- Be Happy
- Be Straightforward
- Just be YOU!

The ability to be who we are meant to be allows us to be unapologetically truthful. We are no longer concerned with what others think because we understand that the essence of who we are resides in our ability to share our authentic selves with the world. Facing reality is not horrific any more because we epitomize realness. Our aura doesn't just say, "take it or leave it," it screams "Accept me, love me, reject me, or hate me… whatever YOU choose I don't give a damn, because I ACCEPT and LOVE me for me.

The benefits of finally embracing YOU means you won't have to lie any more. When I meet people, they are getting all of who I am, not who I am trying to become. When I look in the mirror, I love the person I see (mind, body and spirit). When I hold my boyfriend, I experience a feeling I've never felt before. When I returned home, I could walk with my head up because it no longer mattered if people accepted me or whispered rumors about my past. I released those voices, too. I wasn't expending my energy covering up the lie, but building the life I wanted, but more importantly needed. I'm confident in conversations and daily activities. I have conversations with myself knowing that I am speaking to my soul and truthfully from it as well. I wasn't afraid to face reality anymore. Most of all, I finally have peace about myself and my purpose here on this earth.

So I challenge you to give yourself grace-FULL permission on your journey of acceptance. If it doesn't serve or build you up, release it. If it's something in your past, release it. If it doesn't bring YOU peace or joy, release it. Seek help, YOU are not weak in doing so, you're actually fighting for yourself. You'll appreciate becoming your own advocate, and simply being YOU!

Lesson: Self-acceptance is knowing your weaknesses, strengths and true sense of self-satisfaction. This requires owning your faults, mistakes, and areas of improvement while continuing to love yourself. Additionally, YOU must be willing to let go of everything that doesn't enhance you. This requires recognizing when something or someone is good to YOU and good for YOU. True self-acceptance is finally being OK with the person YOU see in the mirror and loving the reflection.

You don't lose real friends because real friends can never be lost.

~Austin Bergman

Chapter 8

I Wanna Dance with Someone Who Loves Me

O pportunity happens on the dance floor of life, and no matter how ridiculous or cool the dance may look, don't focus on that but focus on what's being achieved! Embrace the vulnerability, joy, and freedom of simply dancing to your own beat. Dancers don't have time to marinate in bullshit or matters that don't enhance their lives because they're too busy living their best lives.

Everybody knows the electric slide, but there are some people that will sit and watch everyone else enjoy and feel the rhythm while they pessimistically ridicule those that have chosen to live. Our lives are not abandoned buildings but an open dance floor that should reveal how much we love life while also allowing us to experience love with the people who surround us. Love is on the dance floor so let the melody woo you as you journey through life… because the best songs are always love songs that lead to a soulful and well-synchronized dance with someone who loves you.

So don't be the wallflower that dies and withers away while scrutinizing the dancers. Be the person who is breaking it down! That's the person dancing as if nobody's watching and the room is completely empty. I have always been *that* guy. However, this requires courage (and maybe a drink or two).

We have to master the ability of not giving a damn about what people think or say about us. Arriving at this place means we are aware that people who judge us don't really know us, and if they do, their opinion, not ours. So don't internalize any of it. Let them have whatever that opinion may be. You just keep dancing and moving to the beat of love!

Speaking of love, it happens naturally. It is never forced and it is always unplanned. Contrary to popular belief love isn't a choice, it is an innate response that is the answer to what we need and desire. Love doesn't possess a certain look; it is "the look."

We all recognize when two people are truly in love as we also recognize when two people despise each other. People who love each other will fight but not with the intent to harm or endanger the other person. People who love each other will exhibit patience in the midst of uncertainty and refuse to abandon their loved-one. People who love each other will let the other person shine and never be intimidated by the light that exudes from the other person/people. People who love focus on bettering themselves and not changing the other person for their benefit, but they change themselves for the better for the continuity of their relationship. People who love each other don't disrespect or devalue each other but they uplift and respectfully accept each other's differences, without ridicule. People who love don't ever seek to just receive love, they desire to give love freely to anyone that needs it and will accept it.

All birds flock together, especially love birds. They sing together, fly together, and most importantly they live and enjoy life, *together*. If we want our lives to be fulfilled we must first center ourselves as a source of love. Then we will attract those who love themselves and in turn they can easily love us, feed us, nurture us, protect us, and live happily ever after with us. Even if they disagree, they know it is temporary because their love is permanent. Although, their song may sound like an off key melody momentarily, they know how to rearrange the melody so it is not just music to their ears, but it translates to their favorite love song that they can dance to forever.

So let's dance with the people who LOVE us, because these people won't attempt to mock our dance moves but they will learn them so they can dance with us. The lovers in our lives are the dancers who won't run from the rain but they will dance in the storm - because they are with us…. *For real!* They won't just dance, but they will also sing… because sometimes we have to dance to our own melody. Especially, when the music of life stops and causes us to freeze unexpectedly. The people who love us will stay with us until the music we love starts again.

My first broker, Linda, is known as the dancing queen. She never chose sides, she loved me when I pretended to be straight, and she loved me even more when I embraced *The Real Austin Bergman*. She was one of the first people I told when coming out. In fact, we were dancing together. I realized in that moment that I was dancing with someone who truly loved me and I loved her because her love is real. She never changed. Even through the ugliness of our divorce, she cared about both me and my ex. She loves us. She is our friend. She is our confidant. More importantly, Linda lives up to her name. She is a beautiful soul - and what is more beautiful than true love and someone who loves beautifully. Thank you Harris for not just understanding me, you've supported me and helped me to be a better person.

Lesson: Center yourself and take control of your playlist and your guest list. Be courageous enough to dance by yourself and also try something new like love. It constantly renews us and others, especially when we deem ourselves worthy of giving and receiving love. So turn up the volume of life and allow love to be the melody that makes you twerk, salsa, line dance and of course, breakdance! Whatever you do, don't STOP the music... that is where life and love reside.

Don't be afraid to start all over again. You might like your new story better.

~ Zach Durham

Chapter 9

Give In & Let Go

As soon as I stopped worrying how I could make life happen, I started living. There are some things we'll have to work at, but worrying shouldn't be one of them. Letting go of our past, fear, doubt, and other people's opinion, liberates us from our own bondage. Thankfully, the BS we experience becomes the fertilizer we need to grow.

Before I came to this realization, I allowed my past mistakes to bury me alive, then I realized it was the nutrients I needed to evolve, excel, and break free! Nothing grows without two things: sunshine and rain...those are given. When we change our perspective, we see challenges as growth and development opportunities. Then there will be times you will assess the situation for what it is and decide that whatever IT is, it is not for me.

Some people cannot have access to you. Access is a privilege not everyone deserves. You're just too good for them and the games they play. Do not allow people to get in your head about who you are and where you're going. This is not being cocky, it is being truthfully intentional about owning your purpose and taking control of your destiny. Don't waste your time because time is something we can't get back.

Sometimes we have to let go of people and things very quickly, especially when we're conscious of what toxic behaviors feel and look like. If it has the potential to be toxic —let it go! If we can relate to it, in a bad way, it's a trigger that could set us back. Remember, when we let go of something or someone, it doesn't mean we're giving up, it means we are assertively stating, "I am doing what is best for me!"

Way too often, we do what's best for others; thereby, living for their applause. Starting today, we must learn to clap for ourselves, see losses as lessons and setbacks as opportunities. There's something to learn in every season of our lives. There's a new lesson because life is the largest classroom and greatest teacher. Pain and triumphs are also teachers that will equip us with drive and hopefully humility. Therefore, as we become older, we can look back and clearly see how we could have done things differently.

Life will humble everyone of us at some point. Whether we're passed up for a promotion, lose our home, lose a business deal or experience rejection at any level, humility will come knocking. The prerequisite of forgiveness is humility. I had to be humiliated to become humble and have the capacity to exercise true forgiveness. I didn't want to spend the rest of my life pouting about my past.

If I would have stopped where I was, my success would have been limited to the past... and I didn't believe I could attain greater success but I have. I was upset with myself for way too long for letting things go so far. I was upset with my ex and I was upset with those who walked away. Then I asked myself, how do I make peace with the mess I've made of my life and with people whom I thought would be there —I had to FORGIVE. I cut my losses and decided to build again, but this time I'd do it on my terms. Whether things went according to plan wasn't my concern... I was only concerned with doing what was best for me, so I let it go, all of it. The weight was finally lifted and I felt light as a floating feather.

True forgiveness is a process and it starts by focusing on YOU. Forgiveness is for our own wellbeing and inner peace. So admit your role in the mess, and forgive yourself. Say your name and what you forgive yourself of. Be brutally honest and if you fucked some things up, say it and vow to never do it again.

We have to acknowledge that sometimes we love people way more than they love us; so, we hold on to them for that reason. Don't fight for anyone to stay, they must desire a space in your life, and their actions will prove as such. Observe the behaviors closely; how they treat you is a direct indication of where you fall on *their* list of priorities... and when they do - YOU must respond accordingly.

We must forgive our perpetrators whether they own anything or not. This is hard, and it is a journey, but we have to do it. If we don't, we will become a victim or a prisoner in our own mind...Free but incarcerated by our thoughts. Remember, forgiveness is about YOUR peace and YOUR freedom. There is no peace when there's a constant retelling of the story in your head or to anyone else who'll listen. Just let it go. We have to release those who hurt us from our hearts by acknowledging that the season of their presence in our lives is up. Say aloud, "I am releasing _____ because it hurts too much to hold _____ in my heart."

Lesson: Just drop it, let it go, and move on! Forgiveness isn't just for you or the other person. Forgiveness is for your future-self —now so you can show up as the real YOU because it is the best YOU. You are worthy of peace and freedom, and it all starts and ends with forgiveness.

For all the doors they slammed on me, I'm coming to buy the entire building.

~ Austin Bergman

Chapter 10

Awwwe So Me = AWESOME

It is YOUR time to BE-YOU-TI-FULL — the irrefutable purpose of being YOU. Nothing is more valuable than being you [originality].

Authentic: YOU must discover who we are, be OK with who YOU are and embrace your authenticity, first, before expecting anyone else to. When YOU come out, some of the thoughts you had will be confirmed and some won't. Just know that YOU have to live with all of who YOU are. Accept the past for what it is, refuse to park there and put your life in drive because your future is where the best days of your life are! Accept this truth and be authentically YOU. Those who love you will also accept YOU, authentically!

Willingness: Be willing to get out of your comfort zone. Comfortability leads to complacency and mediocrity but discomfort will convince YOU that change is necessary. However, in your quest to be YOUR authentic self, you must also willingly accept that everyone will NOT accept YOU, and that is okay!

Embrace: YOU only get one life, embrace all that it has the offer. Embrace change, ups, downs, wins, losses and lessons. Do all the things your heart desires! Leave this planet completely fulfilled because YOU embraced everything the universe threw your way!

Sacred: YOU are sacred. YOU are not for everyone and everyone is not for YOU. Be mindful of who YOU allow in your sacred space and on your sacred journey. God's greatest masterpiece is the creation of humanity. So honor yourself and others, even if it means saying goodbye.

Opportunities: Some opportunities will present themselves, while other times YOU will have to seek them out. However, when opportunities come your way, make sure they align with your personal core values. If you don't have any, set some today. When opportunities align with your core values and who YOU are authentically, expect BIG doors to continue to open (and stay open)!

Meaningful: People may do what we do, but no one else can do it like YOU! At the end of our lives, we must feel that we've completed our assignments with purpose. When YOUR life is meaningful, the need for validation from others is absolutely pointless. So, give YOURSELF a round of applause, and never expect it from anyone else!

Existence: Your existence is more than merely existing, it's being intentional about your happiness. If basket weaving gives YOU peace, then weave the hell out of baskets! As long as YOU are 100 percent satisfied, then your life has meaning.

Lesson: Authentic willingness to embrace sacred opportunities and a meaningful existence. This is AWESOME and so are YOU!

About the Author

Austin Bergman, the Realist and Luxury Real Estate Mogul exudes authenticity! His memoir is an unfiltered disclosure of his past, present, and future. However, he is not ashamed of any of it... because he wouldn't be the Real Austin Bergman without the calamities or the celebrations!

Austin Bergman is renowned for his ability to successfully market and sell Fort Lauderdale's exclusive offerings to the world's wealthy, sophisticated and discerning.

His drive to succeed originates from years of unparalleled personal attention to the high-end real estate industry, researching market trends, innovative ideas, and effective methods to promote and sell his properties locally, nationally, and internationally.

ABOUT THE AUTHOR

Austin is the father of two beautiful girls and being a #GirlDad is his life's joy! In his spare time, he enjoys traveling to undisclosed wonderlands and spending time with people who love life as much as he does!

CPSIA information can be obtained
at www.ICGtesting.com
Printed in the USA
LVHW050114201121
703902LV00010B/343